from Peter for m

# GONE WRITING

GONE   WRITING

# The Poems of
# *Moore on Sunday*

Peter Moore

Foreword by Don Shelby

*University of Minnesota Press*

*Minneapolis*

*London*

Published by the University of Minnesota Press
111 Third Avenue South, Suite 290
Minneapolis, MN 55401-2520
http://www.upress.umn.edu

Cataloguing-in-Publication Data is available from the Library of Congress.

ISBN 0-8166-3432-7

Printed in the United States of America on acid-free paper

The University of Minnesota is an equal-opportunity educator and employer.

11 10 09 08 07 06 05 04 03 02 01 00 99          10 9 8 7 6 5 4 3 2 1

# Contents

D O N   S H E L B Y

# Foreword

Dave Moore loved the word. He loved it spoken in prose, sung in a
tenor voice, and rhymed in lines of poetry. During the thirty-two
years he anchored the news for WCCO-TV, he spoke more words to
more Minnesotans than anyone ever had or ever will. He chose the
words carefully, and he talked us through some very tough times. He
told us of Kennedy's death and the deaths of our sons and our neigh-
bors' sons in Vietnam. He got us through the struggles for civil rights,
and he explained to us the deceit of Watergate. He celebrated our
children's achievements on the field and in the classroom, and he
became, after it all, the most permanently likable and trusted figure
we would ever see in the public light.

  For twenty years I had the wonderful good fortune to work
with Dave. Hundreds of us over the years count as golden time the
days we spent with him. He taught us how to be good journalists and
good citizens. He taught us how to laugh at ourselves and how to take
very seriously the trust given us by the audience. As we watched him
at work, he taught us most frequently how little we knew and how

much we had to learn from him. He managed to do that without ever making us feel small or inconsequential—in fact, just the opposite: one of Dave Moore's most enduring and legendary qualities was his penchant for going out of his way to find kind things to say about the smallest good committed by the least of us.

When he died on January 28, 1998, we were left leaderless. Dave never aspired to leadership—it accrued to him. We called him "The Dean." A newspaper writer had once described him as "the dean of broadcast journalism." Dave was embarrassed by the reference and argued that it was simply not true. "I didn't even go to journalism school," he would often say. We smiled at his protests. He was, to us and very likely to you, the finest journalist we'd ever know.

In 1985 Dave stepped down. His retirement was front-page news for days. The headline of Joe Soucheray's column in the *Pioneer Press* reflected how everyone felt: "Say it ain't so!" It fell to me to take over the 10 P.M. newscast. I tried to explain to one writer what it felt like to move into that role, using an analogy Dave might appreciate. I said I felt like George Selkirk. "Who is George Selkirk?" the writer asked. Selkirk was the guy who replaced Babe Ruth in right field upon the great slugger's retirement. "Never heard of him," said the writer.

Dave was still the newsroom's inspirational leader, and his popular *Moore on Sunday* broadcast continued. There had been many versions of the program; the title changed only by the day of the week on which it aired. But *Moore on Sunday* was the complete Dave Moore. He'd been responsible for some of the best television in the country. In the early years, *The Bedtime Nooz* featured Dave's comic side. The award-winning documentary *Moore Reports* demonstrated Dave's acclaimed journalistic achievements. But the Sunday show gave him a small stage with a large audience and a chance to celebrate the breadth of his talents. Advertising agencies and documentarians had sought Dave's voice for a half-century; it was a well-established fact that no one could vocally interpret a script like Dave could. We had a running joke around the station that if Dave read aloud the script of the worst writer in the building, it would sound like Hemingway had written it. And Dave loved to read nothing so much as poetry. So this book.

From time to time I would look across my desk at Dave and see him reading from a neatly typed paper. His expressive eyes would light up, then he would furl his brow as he read the work in a barely audible voice. This was the way Dave gave life to scripts. We had grown accustomed to his behavior, and sometimes we'd huddle up and without his knowledge watch him work. He would gesture with his hands and suddenly throw his head back and give out a trademark Dave Moore laugh. I wish you could have heard him—it was the kind of laugh that would make you laugh, a cackling wheeze inevitably ending in a sort of exhaustion with his head between his knees.

"Read this," he would say to me when he had caught his breath. "It's Pete's latest contribution." Peter Moore, one of the six talented Moore kids, wrote these most wonderful poems for his father. At first they were just for his dad's amusement, and then one day Dave included a poem in a broadcast. Eventually, Peter's poems were a frequent feature on *Moore on Sunday*. They were always Dave's favorite part of the program and soon the audience began to love them as well.

In this book you will read poems about the subjects Pete knew Dave loved and loved to spoof. You will read a poem extolling the virtues of those chunks of ice that accumulate under the rear fenders of our cars each winter. There are poems here about relationships, holidays, families, and our state. There are poems of recreation and procreation, of children and buildings and most things in between. This book contains one poem that I believe was Dave's personal favorite, a poem that doesn't even qualify as a poem and therein lies its nutty genius.

Something else also commends this book of poems: Peter has given us back the sound of his father's voice. As you read these poems, I hope you hear, as I do, the tinkling of Dave's laughter and the depths of his dramatic tones. I hope you'll hear the cadence, and Dave, I know, would hope you'd hear his pauses. I am grateful to Peter for bringing this book to print. Dave is in here. And for that reason, I'll read and reread this book, as I suspect you will, too.

One of Dave's favorite lines concluded a stanza of an old Irish song. He sang, "Oh, for one more hour of gladness; gone, alas, as our youth too soon." Peter brings Dave back in this book, and the hour of gladness is thankfully ours.

# Preface

For as long as I can remember, humor has been an important (one might almost say defining) element of my life. My parents were voracious readers and very verbal; they instilled in all six of us kids an appreciation for words, wit, and a well-turned phrase, the funnier the better.

Humor was a way of connecting with each other. Quite often at the dinner table my dad would say, "Well, anyone hear any good jokes today?" We'd be off, telling what we'd heard, making up some on the spot, and generally having a good time being together. (Things could get pretty loud, too. Once a playwright friend of mine was visiting while dinner was proceeding at its usual raucous level; he must have looked a little overwhelmed, because my mother said, "What's the matter, John, we too much for you?" He smiled and said, "It's just been a long time since I've been in the midst of such warm chaos.")

During his thirty-two years as the anchorman for the CBS affiliate in Minneapolis, Dad couldn't always make it home for dinner between the 6 and 10 P.M. newscasts, and the evenings he did make it were often the subject of much whining on our parts. (Picture six kids between the ages of two and twelve waiting until seven o'clock for dinner—to this day we all eat like wolves with forks.) But Mom knew how much Dad loved being at that table, and of course he was worth the wait.

My dad had the most wonderful laugh, a high-pitched stacca- to burst of delight that quickly became a near howl before descending into a warm, throaty chuckle (and often ending with a satisfied "Oh, boy!"). Most of the verses in this book were written for his week-in-review news program, *Moore on Sunday* (or as he sometimes called it, "Moron Sunday"). My favorite part of the writing process was calling him up on Wednesday or Thursday and saying, "OK, I think I have something for you," then reading him the new poem and hearing that laugh when I got to the punch line.

Sometimes I'd stop down at WCCO and read the poem to him in person. Invariably when I was finished he'd laugh, shake his head, and say something like, "Aw, Pete, that's terrific, that's just . . . geez, that is so *good*, these verses just *make* this show!" Which of course wasn't remotely true—the program won a bunch of news awards over the years—but his enthusiasm was gratifying and contagious, and I'd walk out of there feeling connected to my dad and like a funny guy to boot.

Not surprisingly, the world has dimmed somewhat for me since Dad's death in January 1998. People tell me that the sadness will diminish with time and I'll get accustomed to not having him around; maybe they're right, I couldn't say. I just know the unique place he held in my life and how lucky I was to have a dad who not only loved me and was proud of me but often told me so.

He used to say he thought he'd failed as a father because he couldn't teach us kids about practical things like power tools or cars or Sheetrock, all the real-world knowledge he knew nothing about. What he did teach us—the value of integrity, the importance of generosity, the joy of humor, and a belief that for the most part the world truly was a benign and wonderful place—has proven in my life to be far more useful. I used to think I gave these poems to him; now I know it was the other way around.

**Peter Moore**

St. Paul, May 1999

# GONE WRITING

# PART I

# The Great (and Not So Great) Outdoors

# A Great Winter Sport

The best part of winter, the best part by far,
Is kicking those ice chunks that form on your car.
No matter our ages or races or genders
We all enjoy booting that slush off our fenders.
It's deeply fulfilling, that contact and sound
Of boot hitting chunk and then chunk hitting ground.
It makes you feel better, it makes your day brighter,
It makes your Tercel about twenty pounds lighter!
And boy, what a workout! We all could be hunks
By starting each morning with kicking some chunks!
So next time you spot one, no matter how awesome,
Don't wait and think maybe you might let it thaw some;
Go after it, mister! Attack it with zeal,
And manfully give it the back of your heel!
It may take you weeks, but of course that's good, too:
The winter goes faster with something to do!

# January in Minnesota

Why do we live here? Why do we stay?
Why don't we leave from October to May?
Surely there must be a logical reason
We stand for this icy, interminable season.
"We're hardy!" say most folks. "We're morons!" say some.
The truth is we're frozen—our brains have gone numb!
So here we sit, shivering, 'til spring plays the hero—
Dreaming of Fahrenheits higher than zero!

# March Once More

Well, we've done it again!
Every March we pretend
That it's spring and the winter is ended.
We ignore that black mound
Of old snow on the ground
So our disbelief's nicely suspended.
Well, I think you'd better
Keep on that nice sweater,
This is MARCH, just in case you've forgotten.
It's not warm, for God's sake,
There's still ice on the lake
(And the swimming, quite frankly, is rotten).
No, you can't say it's spring
'Til the birds do their thing
And the meadows and trees are in flower,
And you put on short pants
'Cause you know there's no chance
Of a twelve-degree drop in an hour!
March is mean, then it's mild,
Like a colicky child
Whose behavior we're always excusing;
And so that's why I say
Don't go out until May,
Which as months go is far less confusing!

# Dayton's Flower Show

I'm not one of those
Who like flower shows.
The sight of a mum
Only makes a heart glum,
And to view a petunia
Can practically ruin ya.
Heartbreakers, liars, deceivers—I know!
They tell us it's spring,
But outside—two below!

# Spring, Sort Of

I get depressed this time of year, when ugly things abound;
The blackened, patchy piles of snow, the landscape dull and brown.
There's trash along the highway that the melted snow's revealed,
And if the sun's inclined to shine that fact is well concealed.
It's too warm for a parka, but a sweater's not enough;
Though baseball's in the news again, it's just spring training stuff.
We're stuck in Nature's waiting room, and Nature can't decide;
Sometimes March is Dr. Jekyll, sometimes Mr. Hyde.
But yesterday I think I saw a tiny tulip bud,
Or else it was a crocus shoot that peeked out through the mud.
And so for now I'll dress in layers and hope that spring comes soon,
While I repeat my favorite words: April, May, and June!

# Oh, the Natural World

It's summer now, and folks all say,
"It's gorgeous! Don't stay in all day!
Let's roam the woods and traipse the fields
And reap the bounty Nature yields!"
Well fine, that's great, go breathe some air,
I'll tell you bluntly, I can't bear
The biting, sucking, crawling things
That gentle summer always brings.
I mostly like what God hath wrought here,
Except for all the bugs He brought here.
And that's reverse psychology
'Cause they seem awfully fond of me!
When I go out on nature trips
The insect world just smacks its lips.
They know me well, I'm much adored,
A five-star insect smorgasbord!
And once they spot me, I've a hunch,
They drop their work and holler, "LUNCH!"
To me, the phrase "The Great Outdoors"
Is code for "Massive Bites and Sores."
I'd love to take an outdoor nap,
But I can't sleep—I mostly slap.
Mosquitoes, with their vasty numbers,
Won't permit alfresco slumbers.

And if by chance the skeeters pass
The other creeps attack en masse.
The wasp, the bee, the flea, the fly,
Chiggers and spiders and ants—oh, my!
But here's a pest to specially note,
Who wins the most repulsive vote.
He's flat and ugly, hard to kill,
His silent bite will make you ill.
Engorged with blood, he's white and fat;
Now what could be more vile than that?
Yes, one word best describes the tick:
Ick.
As far as I'm concerned, all bugs
Are pint-sized, misanthropic thugs,
And I think we should drown in Borax
Anything that has a thorax.
So go ahead—wax hyperbolic
Of rapturous days and joys bucolic;
By Nature I'll remain unsmitten,
And happily stay indoors, unbitten!

# Late Summer Blues

When August arrives, life gets muggy and thick,
Like Nature's been conked on the head with a brick.
The air isn't moving, the sky is all hazy,
My energy level drops well below lazy.
Forget about exercise, workouts are rare;
In August my favorite conditioning is air.
I glisten with sweat, I wear very few clothes
(Which has its advantages sometimes, God knows).
School hasn't started yet, softball is through,
There's nowhere to go and there's nothing to do.
August is boring, August is hot,
August is all the things April is not.
If life were a ball game and I had the ball
I'd intentionally walk August and pitch to the fall.
Yes, August's a drag, but let's always remember:
It still beats the heck out of, say, late November!

# The Hay Fever Rag

I've got allergies, ain't that grand?
You do, too? So you understand.
I cannot breathe or smell or talk,
My head feels like it's filled with caulk.
I took some pills, I drank some soup,
I rubbed on some strange herbal goop,
I sipped hot teas, used nasal sprays,
I inhaled steam for several days.
Old stinky socks, ripe Gorgonzola,
Nothing helped my blocked schnozzola.
And guess what else? When I'm not well
My attitude goes all to hell.
Try speaking clearly—there's a process;
Is "doze" a nap or a proboscis?
Forget fine food: it's such a waste
To eat great things that you can't taste.
God, I'm sure, conceived the sinus
To be a plus and not a minus.
But when I'm clogged with nasal ills
I wish He'd thought to give us gills.

# PART II

# Strikes, Balls, and Lures of the Sporting Life

# Written during the Time of Year Formerly Known as Spring Training

I tried to write a poem last week (a thing I often do);
I wanted something rich and deep, but really funny, too.
But when I called upon my muse for rhymes my fans might like,
She calmly dropped a bombshell, saying, "Sorry, I'm on strike!"
"On strike?" I said. "But you're not real! You're just a mere conceit!"
"That may be so," she sneered, "but even concepts have to eat!
We muses thrive on praise, but you've been stingy with the credit;
And I'm the true creative force, while you just mostly edit!
It takes a pro to find a rhyme for tough words like 'inchoate';
So 'til you share the glory, pal, you're now a museless poet!"
"I'll have your wings for this!" I yelled. "I've been a fair employer!"
She snapped a harp string at me as she left, saying, "Call my lawyer!"
"The hell with her," I thought. "I'll find a good replacement muse;
Some undiscovered fledgling star whose talent I can use."
Well, that was easier said than done—I interviewed for days.
They nearly all had great big dreams and padded résumés.
They begged and pleaded for a chance, some said they'd muse for free,
A few had worked on romance books or sitcoms on TV.
And one had worked for Cupid, helping lonely people mingle;
"I guess I didn't do so hot," she sighed. "They're all still single."
I finally hired a former pro whose harp still seemed in tune;
She once helped write a Bee Gees song and worked for Rod McKuen.

We're doing fine together, though I must admit it's hard;
Her rhythm's just a little bit off, her rhymes a little odd.
Of course I miss my real muse—I'd love to have her back.
It's she who makes my work unique, without her I'm a hack.
I'm certain if we both tried hard we'd find a good solution,
And bring this sordid business to a satisfying conclusion.
But I won't be the first to budge; it's principle, you see:
I'll never let creative thinking get the best of me!

# Opening Day Jive

Here we go! Baseball! Time to play again!
Sittin' in the boxes with a scorecard and a pen, brought
Along a couple buddies, got ourselves a couple beers, say now
I ain't missed an Openin' Day in almost forty years! Yeah, I
Seen 'em when they won it all, I seen 'em when they stank, and I
Seen 'em when the pitching staff went right into the tank! Got a
Rookie here from Portland who they say can do it all, got a
Old guy from the Dodgers who can still shellac the ball! I know
Everybody's number, I know everybody's name, I know
Everythin' there is to know about a baseball game! Gonna
Grab myself a hot dog 'cuz a wiener taste good when you
Eat it to the sound of horsehide flyin' offa wood! And we
Holler at the players and we talk a little ball, and we
Argue who's the best at makin' catches off the wall, say now
Who's that speedy Latin who could turn them double plays, say now
Tell me, don't this Griffey kid look just like Willie Mays? And it's
Two on, two out, what is this, the eighth? If you
Wanna get the batter gotta have a little faith! And it's
Peanuts, popcorn, caramel corn, Coke, hey I
Hope they're gonna win it, but I think they're gonna choke, and it's
Too tense, too much, heart attack time! Well, I'm
Feelin' pretty nervous, but I'm feelin' pretty fine, yeah he
Struck him out! Sat him down! Have another beer! And it's
Too bad Openin' Day can only happen once a year, there ain't

Nothin' like the feelin' that you get from bein' here, and it's
Too bad Openin' Day can only happen once a year, and it's
Too bad Openin' Day can only happen once a year!

# On Mother's Day and the Fishing Opener Falling on the Same Day

If you woke up this chilly morn and thought, "Let's fish!"—think twice.
Both morally and physically, you're probably on thin ice.
I know that nothing rivals Opening Day for angling drama,
But keep in mind it's Mother's Day and what you owe your mama.
Who gave you your first rod and taught you how to calmly wait?
Who showed you all the subtleties of how to use live bait?
She bought you your first tackle box, she made you practice trolling,
Yes, she was right there on the dock when other moms went bowling!
She loved you, man, and now that she's too old to fish herself,
You've left her all alone like some stuffed lunker on the shelf!
It's not too late to let her know your love is still afloat . . .
So bring along that mobile phone—we'll call her from the boat!

# Move It

You say the baseball strike's a drag;
The hockey strike is, too.
The sports page of your daily rag
Is now so thin it's see-through.
You say these slimy legal guys
Have killed the world of sports,
And all the losses, wins, and ties
Now happen in the courts.
You say we sports fans have it tough,
This lack of games is gruesome.
Well, I say, hey, get off your duff—
Quit watching sports and do some!
Let's hit some balls, let's ride a bike,
Let's dribble, swim, or run
(Don't tell me I should take a hike;
I'd say that sounds like fun!).
You say you're old and fat and slow
And highly unathletic;
Well, trust me, if you play I know
You'll feel much less pathetic!
So grab a racquet, get your glove,
And so what if you botch it;
Sports for me is just like sex:
I'd rather do than watch it!

# Heartbreak

You ask me why I'm feeling bad, you ask me why I'm blue,
You ask me if I'm eating right
Or if I have the flu.
You ask me if my inner child is unfulfilled and cries.
You ask me if I need to get
Some outdoor exercise.
You ask me why I can't enjoy this autumn so resplendent.
You ask me quietly if I've met
Some leggy flight attendant.
You ask me if I'm in despair about some global crisis,
The disappearing forests
Or the rise in oil prices.
I know you want to help but you can never understand
This emptiness, this sense of grief
Known only to a man.
So here's my answer to your kind and well-intentioned queries:
I feel a deep abiding loss . . .
I miss the damn World Series.

# Kirby Puckett's Retirement

I think it was Freud who said nothing's enjoyed
To its fullest until it's recalled;
And so let's reminisce about all that we'll miss
And just why this guy kept us enthralled.
His first claim to fame was his musical name,
A children's song, rhythmic and fun.
And that kidlike physique, so compact and unique,
That could do things that couldn't be done.
We all saw his fire, his guts and desire,
But the thing we sensed watching him play
Was this overgrown kid really loved what he did;
He had fun at his job every day.
So remember his muscle, his talent and hustle,
Remember each homer he blasted.
Let's shed no more tears, we had thirteen great years,
And oh, man—was it fun while it lasted!

# Some Thoughts on
# the End of Fishing Season

The fishing season's come and gone, and anglers, please take note:
We poets scoff at those who spent their weekends in a boat!
There's not a special art to catching walleye, trout, or herring,
But poetry requires a ton of patience, skill, and daring!
You have to rise at 3 A.M., a dark and quiet time;
No noise or lights to scare away your fragile sense of rhyme.
You need a special pen, of course (I like the five-inch Parker);
A Bic is fine for sonnets, but haiku needs Magic Marker.
You then go to your secret spot, your favorite writing hole,
And hope those words you know are down there rise up from your soul.
And then the real excitement hits! God knows there's nothing sweeter
Than reeling in big images that scan in perfect meter!
And when you've rhymed your limit and your rhythm's finally done,
You meet up with your poet pals for real iambic fun!
You tell the same old stories, like the one about the day
You thought you'd found a rhyme for "orange" but then it got away!
Or how you wrote your epic with a plain old ballpoint pen,
Then had it framed and mounted on the fireplace in your den!
Yes, poetry's a glamorous thing, that just can't be denied;
It brings a spark of fun to life that fishing can't provide.
So keep your boring rods and reels, your tales of crappies biting;
I've closed up shop and on my door I've hung a sign: GONE WRITING!

# Ah, the Holidays

# Watching Schoolchildren See a Live Turkey for the First Time

I'm a turkey, nice to meet ya,
Step in closer, I won't eat ya.
That's just a common courtesy
I wish that you'd extend to me.
Right now you think I'm such a sweetie,
But you're the eater, I'm the eatee.
Don't say we're friends, it's too depressing.
Friends don't serve their friends with dressing.
Thanksgiving dinner's all I am
So no more questions. Beat it. Scram!

# A Midwestern Thanksgiving

A question to set the mind reeling:
Why *do* we find Jello appealing?
It's tacky and cheap, a shivering heap
Of sugary substance congealing.

But the answer, without being rude,
Is that Jello can alter our mood.
For in theory and practice,
The plain simple fact is
We all like to play with our food.

O how it quivers, O how it quakes,
O what a huge heaping portion it makes!
Whether red, green, or yellow, with carrots or not,
The folks here at home sure do eat it a lot.
And why do we like it so much? Here's a notion:
It's thrilling to eat a dessert still in motion!

# Post-Thanksgiving Musings

This Thursday past no doubt you ate
The splendors heaped upon your plate:
The steaming soups, the candied yams,
The basted birds and honeyed hams,
The crème brûlée and rhubarb pies
Brought forks to lips and tears to eyes.
And yet, amidst this wondrous fare,
These answers to a gourmand's prayer,
The lowly squash is hands-down winner
Of "Things I Love the Best for Dinner."
It isn't trendy, hip, or posh
To sing the praises of the squash;
I know it's not a glamorous viand
Like chocolate mousse or Chateaubriand.
But it's a shame this tasty gourd
Is much maligned and oft ignored.
I'm well aware its shape and texture
Leave it open to conjecture,
But oh, that smell, that vibrant taste
By gastronomes must be embraced!
The squash is dinner's crowning glory,
The height of good things gustatory!
I realize you slaves to fashion
May not share my squashy passion

And will, I'm sure, keep going goo-goo-la
Over star fruit and arugula.
I'm certain time will rearrange
How food's perceived and things will change,
And squash will be what man adores!
But 'til that day . . . can I have yours?

# On Noticing That No One Ever Gets the Lyrics Right to "Good King Wenceslas" or Most Other Christmas Carols

Forgot the lyrics? No big thing:
The words aren't that appealing.
It's not important *what* you sing
As long as it's with feeling.

Good King Wenceslas just grins;
He could not be prouder.
He forgives our lyric sins
If we all sing louder.

So let 'er rip and have no fear,
Just let that song go ringing,
Because the point this time of year
Is just to be there singing!

# 'Tis the Season

That time of year has come again,
And much as it appalls,
We usually sane and cautious men
Will head out to the malls.
It's time to join the shopping race;
Bring wallet, spouse, and kiddies,
And hope we find a parking space
That's still within the cities.
The store's a madhouse, wild as hell,
It's shopping in flagrante!
The people writhe and moan and yell
Like something out of Dante.
"Do you have this in red or teal?"
"Is that an extra-large?"
"Do you think this has sex appeal?"
"Will that be cash or charge?"
The whole thing's gotten so absurd,
A twisted plot of Satan's;
It makes me wish I'd never heard
Of Macy's, Sears, or Dayton's.
So fa-la-la and all that crap
This shopping stuff's a bummer;
How 'bout we all just take a nap
And not wake up 'til summer?

# A Yuletide Prayer

Preserve us, Lord, this holiday
From clods who would a glass uphold,
And at the table drone away
While all that lovely food gets cold.

O grant us, Lord, a gracious host
Who keeps his blessing short and sweet,
And knows full well a perfect toast
Should finish with the words, "Let's eat!"

# A New Year's Judgment

For those of us much disinclined to revel New Year's Eve,
We marvel at what you call fun; one almost can't believe.
No doubt you found some large soirees in places unaesthetic,
Packed tight with boring, common folk—how dreary, how pathetic.
You gorged yourself on fattening foods, cold shrimp and tortellini,
And probably clogged an artery with all that clam linguine.
You laughed so loud and drank so much you could have had a
    blackout,
And goodness knows, the way you danced you probably threw your
    back out.
And then at midnight, I've no doubt, all heedless of the danger,
You got into a lip-lock with some tall, attractive stranger!
Well, not for me, such lewd displays, such vulgar goings-on;
I went to bed at eight that night, while you caroused 'til dawn.
For mine's a soul above all that, not sensuously delighted;
Although I must confess—just once, I'd like to be invited.

# Considering New Year's Resolutions— Again

Nobody knows where the old year goes,
But the new one is here once again.
And on January first, in a pious outburst,
We resolve to be much better men.

We all swear to lose weight and to not sleep late
And in general renounce all our vices.
But it's kind of like shopping without ever once stopping
Just to take a quick peek at the prices.

Because virtue ain't cheap, it'll cost you some sleep
As you sneak down the stairs for a smoke;
Or you have a piece of pie and you think with a sigh,
"That's the fourth resolution I've broke."

So you go from bad to worse and you mutter and you curse
And it's all just a pain in the neck.
So instead of trying to fake 'em, I'm just not gonna make 'em—
Live an imperfect life, what the heck!

# Hopes for the New Year

The old year is finished, the new one's begun,
And since it's still early you might find it fun
To dream up a list, either long or petite,
Of what you might do this year, who you might meet.
You might learn to dance (you'll be glad you did later).
You might meet Madonna and casually date her.
You might write a screenplay, a lighthearted romance,
Produce it for peanuts and clean up at Sundance!
You might get discovered and move to L.A.,
Call everyone "Babe" and drink decaf au lait.
You then might become Cindy Crawford's new beau
(She recently split up with Richard, you know).
She'll be so impressed as you find cures for cancer;
"He's smart!" she'll tell friends. "And my God, what a dancer!"
Bill Clinton might call you and ask for advice
On how to make Congressman Gingrich play nice.
So you'll holler at Newt and you'll make him behave,
Then you'll go on the *Late Show* and trade quips with Dave!
You might save the whales and then wipe out world hunger,
And find ten great ways to stay fit and look younger!
There's no telling what might transpire this year,
So face it with fire and courage, not fear!
You just might get lucky, you just might get hot,
And all this might happen . . .
But probably not.

# Once More into the New Year's Breach

At last I've made some resolutions,
New Year's Day—inspired solutions
To the many faults that haunt me,
Like these rolls of fat that taunt me,
Like my hair, my breath, my skin,
The general mess my life is in.
So no more sleeping late for me,
And no more pizza, no more Brie!
I'll rise at 6 (6:10 at most)
And start each day with dry wheat toast.
I'll exercise a thousand ways:
Lift weights, do sit-ups, jog for days.
I'll shun dessert and nightly feast
On tofu, kelp, and brewer's yeast.
And if I keep it up each week
I'll be a hunk and not a geek.
My life will be a wondrous thing,
All thanks to resolution-ing!
So come on, sluggards, every one,
Make up a list as I have done,
Indulge a while in its caprices,
Then tear it into little pieces
And use the scraps for starting fires:
We may be fools—but we're not liars!

# PART IV

# Familial Foibles

# On Announcing for the First Time in Your Life That You Won't Be at Your Parents' House on Christmas Morning

It's hard sometimes to be autonomous
And keep things with your mom bonhomonous.

# To All the Brand New Husbands

Romance was born the day we met, the fates brought us together;
We drank champagne, wrote odes to love, and had some fun with leather.
But I noticed once we married and I moved into her place
That our thundering, swirling passions thundered at a slower pace.
So I said, "You've seemed so angry since the day that I moved in,
And I hardly ever see you flash that wicked little grin.
I'd do anything to fan the flame, refill our loving cup."
She said, "Honest?" I said, "Yes." She said, "All right, then listen up:
Light a candle in the bathroom, leave the seat down when you're done,
Push your chair in, turn the lights off, wipe the counter, every crumb.
Raise the blinds up in the morning, pull them down again at night,
And I'll be your little lamby-kins when everything is right.
Take your elbows off the table, take the bathmat off the floor,
Take your shoes off in the kitchen, shut that open closet door.
And when everything is straightened up and all the work is done,
Then I'll shoot you that come-hither look and say, 'Let's have some fun!'
Have you noticed, you big lummox, that I'm doing all the work?
So I fume and get resentful, and then *I* look like the jerk!
If you want things to be different, here's a simple rule, my dear:
When you notice something's dirty, grab a sponge and not a beer!
Don't leave laundry on the door frame, don't wash stemware by the neck,
Take the cans out for recycling, it's politically correct.
Keep the thermostat at sixty-one, it really isn't cold,
And I'll warm your little buns myself sometime before we're old!"

Well, I stared in mute amazement, then I leapt up with a shout
And I did the dishes, cleaned the stove, and took the garbage out.
And since then I've gladly cleaned the house, it gives my life a lift;
'Cuz now everything gets polished, if you kinda catch my drift.
So to all you brand new husbands: pay attention, stop and think.
Pick your socks up, fold the laundry, use the toilet, not the sink.
Because that's what they find sexy, not just being tall or lean;
To be truly irresistible—make sure the sheets are clean!

# Wisdom

Here's a fact that married folks should know about sex:
Too much, you have a baby; not enough, you have an ex.

# The Week after Labor Day

A special sound is in the air,
A lovely noise, unique and rare;
That gentle roar we've all been hearing
Is fifty million parents cheering.
It's clear what's made them so lighthearted:
The simple fact that school has started!
They've hugged and kissed the little tykes
And sent them off on bus and bikes
To learn and grow and do their best
And give their frazzled folks a rest.
They love their kids, make no mistake,
But boy, it's nice to have a break.
Five days each week, from 8 'til 3,
It's kind of great to be kid-free.
That's why, when they come charging home
Like Mongols bent on sacking Rome,
Folks sigh and think, "Well, there goes *my* day!"
And thank their stars it isn't Friday.
Of course that's not the sort of thing
That one should *say* to one's offspring.
You say, "I missed you!" and yes, that's so—
But just how much, they'll never know!

# My Beautiful New Niece

Zosha Kenya Winegar Schultz.
A lovely child, she has no faults,
Except her long and complex name
For which her parents are to blame.

*Dave Moore's high school graduation photo from Minneapolis Washburn High School, 1942.*

*Dave with sons Charlie, Andy, and Peter, 1958.*

*In the booth at WTCN, soon to become WCCO, in the early 1950s.*

*As Ensign Pulver (far right) in Mr. Roberts at the Old Log Theater, 1951.*

*An early publicity shot for the 10:00 P.M. news.*

*Dave in front of the former home of WCCO in 1954.*

*On the air with Clellan Card, host of the popular kids' show* Axel and His Dog.

*The two most trusted faces on Twin Cities television.*

*Reporting election returns with radio news icon Cedric Adams.*

*Dave and his son Peter ham it up
for a public television fundraising
campaign in 1988.*

*Dave celebrating with Don Shelby
after receiving WCCO's Dorr Award
in 1994.*

# More Wisdom

Women will always forgive men their faults
If (a) they do housework and (b) learn to waltz.

# My Wife's Birthday

If love is like water, then I'm not an ocean;
It's lonely and empty and always in motion.
Nor am I a glacier, all frozen and hard,
That takes fifty years to move forward a yard.
I can't be a dewdrop—too youthful and callow.
I could be a puddle, but then I'd be shallow.
I might be the rainfall on soft summer nights,
But that wouldn't work 'cause I'm too scared of heights.
It isn't romantic, but I like to think
Of myself as the leak in an old kitchen sink.
It's often annoying and gets on your nerves,
And wants more attention than plumbing deserves,
But wouldn't you miss it if—poof—it were gone?
It's steady as sunset, as certain as dawn.
There's comfort in hearing that wet little slap
As the drops gently fall to the sink from the tap.
It's constant, dependable, day in day out;
And isn't that really what love's all about?
For what in the world could be more reassuring
Than knowing there's something in life that's enduring?
So don't call the plumber; it's there for a reason,
To tell you you're loved, every day, every season.
Just turn on the faucet and take a big sip:
Happy Birthday, my love, from your favorite drip!

PART V

# The Cultural Life

# On Seeing the World's Largest Book, According to Guinness

Holy smokes! Is that a *book*?
Move over there, let's take a look:
It weighs a ton, the print is small,
There ain't no pictures here at all!
It figures that those nerds at Guinness
Would love a book no one can finish.
You well-read types may think it's groovy,
But I'll just wait and see the movie.

# Thoughts on the Opening of the Frederick R. Weisman Art Museum

Have you seen the Weisman?
It's really a nice one!
If buildings were football, I'd give it the Heisman!

It glistens and curves,
It bulges and swerves,
It gets on a lot of the Lutherans' nerves.

They gasp and say, "Golly!
An architect's folly!
Mies van der Rohe teamed up with Salvador Dali!

It's ugly! It's cold!
Too daring! Too bold!
It's bad for our youngsters! It frightens our old!"

They'll holler and whine
About the design
But once some time passes they'll like it just fine.

For despite shows of piety
And outward sobriety
Even Norwegians enjoy some variety.

So let 'em all fuss
For it's always been thus:
First we shape our buildings and then they shape us.

# Wisconsin Names the Polka as State Dance and Twenty-Second State Symbol

Sound the horns and strike the tabors!
Hail to thee, O eastern neighbors!
Your great Wisconsin legislature
Has changed the course of man and nature.
With sinews stiff, they've risked a chance
And named the polka your state dance!
They dealt first with minutiae,
Like highways, schools, and bills to pay,
Then passed this bill so bold and fateful,
Making tuba players grateful!
Let Rio keep its carioca,
Madison's endorsed the polka!
Those legislators, deft and nimble,
Have nabbed another fine state symbol.
They have a bird, they have a beer,
They have a sandwich (grilled cheese, we hear).
They have a song (no doubt sublime),
But mostly, I think, they have too much free time!

# Ethnic Cuisine

Your average Malaysian
Needs little persuasion
To eat spicy dishes;
He finds them delicious.

An East Indian child
Finds curry quite mild
And consumes fiery chutney
To the point we'd call gluttony.

At hot food a Thai
Probably won't bat an eye,
And of course the Chinese
Eat whatever they please.

But I'm Minnesotan,
Where spice is verboten;
And that's why hot chilies
Just give me the willies.

# A Dissenting Voice

I hate the State Fair! That's shocking, I know,
But, really—why *would* any nice person go?
Though the size of the crowd in itself is dumbfounding
The size of the folks *in* the crowd is astounding!
The grounds are a mess and the buildings are crude,
But the worst thing about it, of course, is the food.
Those donuts and cheese curds are fragrant illusions:
They're really deep-fried coronary occlusions!
Just listen: you'll hear, as you fill up your gut,
The sound of your arteries all snapping shut!
The Grandstand is tacky, the Midway's a rip-off
(Tattoo-covered vendors are always a tip-off).
The annual exhibit of art made of plants
Is probably why Congress stopped NEA grants.
The carousel's fine, though the horses need dusting,
But bungee jumps? Butter queens? Please—how disgusting!
The Fair is immoral, there's all kinds of sin there;
Of course, I'm just guessing, since I've never been there.
I'm told if I went I'd have fun, but I doubt it:
I might have to give up complaining about it!

# PART VI

# Breaking News

# Sweeps Month

If you should choose to watch the news
Remember it's sweeps month—watch out for the ooze!

The month when each station can cause a sensation
And good taste is sent on a four-week vacation.

Just turn on the set; I'm willing to bet
The sizzling reporting will make your teeth sweat!

"ON-THE-JOB SEX BLAMED FOR FATAL TRAIN WRECKS!"

"MOTHER TERESA CAUGHT PASSING BAD CHECKS!"

"WE'LL MEET SISTER FAY, WHO AUTHORITIES SAY
IS RUNNING A BROTHEL JUST SOUTH OF CLOQUET!"

"THE DWARVES—ALL SEVEN—SAY SNOW WHITE WAS HEAVEN;
SHE'S SUING FOR DAMAGES—FILM AT ELEVEN!"

It makes me feel sleazy and clammy and queasy
But turning the silly thing off isn't easy.

For I have to say, in some comforting way,
Sweeps month assures me my own life's okay.

It's kind of a yawn, no wild goings-on,
But who needs reporters camped out on the lawn?

So let the sweeps be, I'll watch blissfully,
Just grateful the broadcasts are not about me!

# On the Publication of a Report That Says Most People Don't Wash Their Hands after Going to the Bathroom

So this researcher's shocked that our hygiene is bad;
Big deal—here's what *really* appalls:
The thought of some guy with a pencil and pad
Taking notes while he hides in the stalls!

I think we're just lazy, we're not really slobs,
And I sure hope this guy understands
That most of our mothers did pretty good jobs
And taught us: Don't pee on your hands!

# "NWA Seeks Casino in the Sky"
## —*Star Tribune* Headline

High-altitude gaming! An airborne casino!
It's kind of redundant from everything *we* know.
If you like taking chances whenever you ramble
Then flying Northwest by itself is a gamble.
Will the plane land on time? Will it be the right town?
Will they go out of business before we touch down?
And how could a video jackpot compare
To bouncing white-knuckled through turbulent air?
They say it's to help us get through the long haul,
But it's just one more way to get back at us all.
It's subtle, but nasty, the ultimate hurt:
Along with your luggage, you can now lose your shirt.

# The Buzz around the Mall

The Megamall's announced a test:
They're using wasps to battle pests!
The bugs are bad, but hey, no prob,
These macho wasps can do the job.
Well, maybe normal wasps could, *but*—
These guys have had their stingers cut!
Now, I'm no shrink but there's no doubt
A gelded wasp has lost his clout.
He's born to sting and if he can't
He's just a wimpy flying ant!
He'll hang his head in deep embarrassment,
Quite uninclined toward insect harassment.
The price of Hugedale's pest-free dream
Is loss of waspy self-esteem.
The bugs know this—you think they'd care
If eunuch wasps invade the air?
(And by the way, where would you get a
Stingless wasp? Palm Springs? Wayzata?)
I hope it works, but boy, I'm tense.
Does fighting bugs with bugs make sense?
Who wants to be where pests abound?
The heck with this—let's shop downtown!

## "Pelicans and Power Lines Don't Mix, Granite Falls Officials Find"
## —*Star Tribune* Headline

The pelican's a funny bird,
The body slim, the beak absurd;
He glides and soars to heights divine
And then takes out a power line.
And this has happened more than once,
So is this bird a total dunce?
Well, I think not; it seems quite clear
He's sent a message we should hear.
By knocking out your TV show
He's saying, "Off your butt! Let's go!
Don't sit inside! Don't watch TV!
You'll learn a lot more watching me!"
With almost genius-like invention
He's telling us to pay attention.
So if we stay indoors all summer,
He may be dumb—but we'd be dumber.

# Earth Mom

It's Earth Day again, our yearly reminder
To treat this old world a bit gentler and kinder.
You've heard this before, but the earth's like your mother;
She just hopes you're happy, she won't be a bother,
She knows you're so busy with big deals that thrill you,
But, really, a call now and then—would it kill you?
As long as she isn't completely forgotten
She'll gladly forgive you for treating her rotten.
So keep this in mind (as truths go, there's none greater):
Ignore your mom now, and you'll be sorry later!

# Election Day

I'm not going to write about this year's election;
No pithy bon mots, no witty dissection
Of ugly campaigning and badly done ads
Depicting opponents as liars and cads.
No sharp, funny send-ups of power and greed;
To put it quite bluntly, there's simply no need.
The daggers of satire can stay on the shelves
Since all of the candidates skewered themselves.
No bright, clever rhyme scheme could be half as funny
As watching politicos try to raise money
Or strive to convince us they're honest and good
While bearing a striking resemblance to wood.
Their mudslinging battles get downright hilarious
Especially when polls show their lead is precarious.
Denials and evasions become so abundant
To satirize that is just flat-out redundant.
This process, no doubt, would be far more amusing
If not for the fact that it's goofballs we're choosing
To make big decisions, to write and pass laws,
And once you stop laughing it does give you pause.
So why bother writing things comic or silly
When clearly I'd only be gilding the lily.

And here's one more reason I will not wax humorous
About politicians whose faults are so numerous.
Election Day proved what I've always suspected:
Too many political jokes get elected.

# The Last Word

I've learned a lot about myself through all these many years;
I've had my share of laughter and I've had my share of crying.
And of the many things that bring me untold joy in life,
Like having friends I treasure and a warm and loving spouse,
I find that writing poetry remains my heart's delight;
Had I the time I'd just write verses morning, noon, and evening.
So many things inspire me, like a lovely night in June;
The soft, romantic midnight light that shines down from the sky.
Or maybe it's the kitten I saw playing with a ball,
Or possibly the mighty oak so towering and so huge.
I only write for fun, of course; I'm hardly Keats or Shelley,
My words don't dance across the page like Nureyev or Fred Astaire.
And though I think my verbal skills are quite refined and good,
I've always found it difficult to rhyme things like I ought to.
But still, before my time is up, before my race is run,
I hope to see my poems in print someday before I'm finished.
Despite some flaws I like to think I have a certain style,
A warm and puckish sort of charm that makes the reader grin.
And maybe some big publisher will find them deep and funny;
They'll sell a million copies and they'll make me lots of friends.
But 'til that day I'll hone my skills and calmly sit and wait,
And read my work to friends who say, "We think your poems are good!"

D A V E   M O O R E   anchored WCCO-TV newscasts for thirty-four years in his hometown of Minneapolis, retiring in 1985 to host the week-in-review news program *Moore on Sunday*, which ran until 1997. He is affectionately remembered for his Saturday night satire on the news, *The Bedtime Nooz* (which ran from 1962 to 1971), a show that featured his fine acting ability and irrepressible sense of humor. Moore died in 1998 at the age of 73.

P E T E R   M O O R E   has worked as an actor and director in theater and film for more than twenty years. He has performed Off-Broadway in New York, with the Guthrie Theater in Minneapolis, in several feature films, and in countless commercials.

D O N   S H E L B Y   has worked for WCCO-TV since 1978 and currently anchors the 6 P.M. and 10 P.M. news. He was a protégé of Dave Moore for nearly twenty years. While at WCCO-TV, Don has won three national Emmys and has twice been awarded the George Foster Peabody, the broadcast equivalent of the Pulitzer Prize. He has been honored as the Dr. Martin Luther King Jr. Humanitarian of the Year and was recognized with the Great American Traditions Award by B'nai Brith.